ALL ACCESS
KEKE PALMER

ALL ACCESS KEKE PALMER

By Riley Brooks

SCHOLASTIC INC.

New York   Toronto   London   Auckland   Sydney
Mexico City   New Delhi   Hong Kong   Buenos Aires

© 2009 by Scholastic

ISBN-13: 978-0-545-17590-6
ISBN-10: 0-545-17590-9

Published by Scholastic Inc.
SCHOLASTIC and associated logos are trademarks and/or registered
trademarks of Scholastic Inc.

12 11 10 9 8 7 6 5 4 3 2 1   9 10 11 12 13 14/0

Designed by Deena Fleming
Printed in the U.S.A.
First printing, June 2009

CONTENTS:

Introduction

It was a beautiful spring day on April 20, 2006, at the Academy of Motion Pictures, where a crowd had gathered to watch the arrival of some very popular stars for a film premiere. The movie was *Akeelah and the Bee*, a small picture that was generating very big buzz. *Akeelah and the Bee* is all about a young girl from a bad neighborhood who defies the odds, to advance through spelling bee after spelling bee, to make it to the Scripps National Spelling Bee. The red carpet that afternoon was graced with well-known stars from the cast like Laurence Fishburne, Angela Bassett, Erica Hubbard, and Curtis Armstrong. Stars like Tyler Perry and Anika Noni Rose were also in attendance to catch the first screening of the film. But by far the most anticipated star of the evening was perhaps the least well-known. Everyone was waiting to see the breakout young actress who had brought Akeelah to life — Keke Palmer.

Keke finally arrived to flashes of cameras as she stepped out onto the red carpet. The thirteen year old was dressed in a strapless cream-colored dress with a black lace overlay and a flirty, full skirt. She had her long dark hair tied in a low, side ponytail and was wearing a gold bracelet and a pinky ring. A lot of young girls would have been overwhelmed walking down that red carpet with reporters and fans yelling to grab their attention and cameras flashing left and right, but not Keke. She took her time, answering questions from reporters, posing for pictures, and greeting fans, and she loved every minute of it. Everyone there that night could see that Keke was born to be a star. Her natural charisma and beauty shone for everyone to see as she was ushered into the theater to watch her movie on the big screen.

As the lights came up at the end of the screening, everyone turned to look at Keke. They had heard that she was good, but they were blown away after seeing it for themselves. Keke had utterly and completely stolen the show from some of the biggest names in Hollywood, and there was no doubt in anyone's mind that she had a very bright future in front of her. How do you spell "super-star"? That night, everyone in the audience was spelling it K-E-K-E P-A-L-M-E-R.

CHAPTER 1:
Enter Lauren Keyana Palmer

When Sharon and Lawrence met in a theater class in college, they had no idea that their daughter would one day become a seriously famous actress. But the two did know that they had some intense chemistry — it was love at first sight. Sharon and Lawrence were married shortly after their college graduation and moved to Chicago to pursue theater careers. They both found work at the prestigious Black Ensemble Theater where they wowed crowds every night. Then, in 1991, Sharon gave birth to their first child, a little girl they named L'Oreal Palmer. Sharon and Lawrence loved being parents. So much so, that they decided to have another baby. In 1993, L'Oreal Palmer found out that she was going to have a baby sister. L'Oreal had an imaginary friend named Keke and she was determined to convince her parents to name her new little sister Keke too, but her parents had other ideas. On August 26, when Sharon gave birth in Harvey, Illinois, the Palmers decided to name the new baby Lauren Keyana. But since L'Oreal refused to call her new little sister anything except Keke, the nickname stuck pretty quickly!

From the start, it was clear that Keke was a born performer. Of course, no one was surprised since her parents were both actors. Keke and L'Oreal spent a lot of time growing up at the Black Ensemble Theater where their parents performed. They hung out backstage, in dressing rooms, the orchestra pit, and the lighting booth. Little Keke loved the excitement and hustle and bustle of every show. She got to see how actors honed their skills and she really developed an appreciation for acting as a craft. Keke probably uses techniques she learned from the stage actors at the Black Ensemble Theater in her film and television work today. Keke learned more during that time than anyone probably guessed back then. In fact, despite landing numerous roles, Keke has never taken a single acting class. "I didn't want to take acting lessons because I don't think anyone can teach you how to act," she told *Black Star News*. "You have to find that in yourself."

Growing up, Keke lived with her family in Robbins, Illinois, a town once known as the Harlem of the Midwest. It is the hometown of many notable African Americans, including actress Nichelle Nichols, basketball player Dwayne Wade, football player Joe Montgomery, and businessman Samuel B. Fuller. Fuller was the first millionaire in Robbins, and he mentored John H. Johnson, who founded the Johnson Publishing Company. The Johnson Publishing Company publishes the African American interest magazines *Jet* and *Ebony*, which has featured Keke in its glossy pages! From 1930–33, Robbins was the home of the first airport in the United States to be run by African Americans. In this vibrant and supportive community, the talented Keke began to shine at a young age.

The Palmer family was very involved in their local church and Keke's mother was a talented soloist in the church choir. Sharon has always loved singing and making music — she even had Lawrence build her a recording studio in their house! Keke loved watching her mom sing in the choir every Sunday, and she couldn't wait to join herself. Finally, when she was five years old, Keke convinced her mother to let her sing with the church choir. Given a chance, Keke didn't just hang back and sing in the chorus — she did a solo of the hymn "Jesus Loves Me." Even then, she knew how to choose a song that would command attention. The entire congregation was blown away by Keke's powerful pipes. Sharon could tell how dedicated her daughter was to singing, and she worked with Keke in their recording studio to help her improve. That time spent with her mom really helped Keke decide that she wanted a career in music. Keke told *The Hollywood Reporter*, "My mom did singing. We always played instruments in the basement. So, I always knew I'd do something in the entertainment business." Her parents never stopped encouraging Keke to reach for her dreams, even though they knew that very few people ever become stars in the entertainment world. They also set an amazing example for Keke by following their own dreams but also working hard to provide for their family, and never giving up — even when times were tough! "My parents are my role models. All they've done for me, they're just major people in my life. They've stood by me and got me where I am today," Keke told PBSKids.org.

When Keke was eight years old, her supportive family became even bigger when her mom gave birth to fraternal twins. Keke and L'Oreal got a new brother and a new sister! Sharon and Lawrence named the twins Lawrence and Lawrencia after their dad. Sharon and Lawrence had both retired from the acting world so that they could spend more time at home with their family. After all, raising kids when you have to work nights and weekends for rehearsals and performances would be tough. Lawrence had gotten a job working for a polyurethane company and Sharon had become a high school teacher who specialized in working with autistic children. Their new jobs meant that Sharon and Lawrence were home more often and got to spend plenty of time nurturing their children, but they never gave up entirely on their love of performing. So when Keke was drawn to the spotlight, they were right there to encourage her.

For the next few years, Keke continued to sing and acted in school productions. When she was nine, Sharon saw an advertisement in the local newspaper for auditions for the stage production of *The Lion King*. Keke recalled to *The Hollywood Reporter*, "My mom asked me if I wanted to do it, and I said, 'Of course' — because I love to sing, I love to dance. So, I'd maybe try to act.

My dad took me to the place where they had auditions at — this was in Chicago, the touring production — and I made it down to the top 15, and then I was out. I was like, 'I like how this goes down. I want to keep at it.' My mom said, 'This will be a fun little hobby thing.' So, she found me an agent." A lot of kids would have been disappointed to have worked so hard only to be cut at the very end, but Keke loved the challenge and was excited to go to more auditions.

Right around the time that Keke signed with the agent, there were open auditions in Chicago for a reality television singing competition called *American Juniors*. *American Juniors* was a spinoff of the adult reality show *American Idol*. The *American Juniors* contestants were children from across the United States. They auditioned in Los Angeles, Chicago, and New York for judges Gladys Knight, Deborah Gibson, and Jordan Knight of the popular 1980's band New Kids On the Block. Instead of the viewers voting contestants off until one person was named the winner of the show, the young contestants were vying to be voted into a group of five. These five kids would record and perform together as a pop act.

Keke's first audition for *American Juniors* was successful. Her strong voice and adorable smile really impressed the judges. She continued on in the competition, flying to Los Angeles as one of the top 60 contestants. The other singers in the competition included Jordan McCoy, who is currently signed to Diddy's label Bad Boy Records, Lucy Hale, who stars on the CW television show *Privileged*, and Katelyn Tarver, who is now a Wilhelmina model and pop singer. While in Los Angeles, Keke's second audition placed her in the top 33. But when the top 20 was announced, Keke was out. She never made it on camera, but the producers assured her that they wanted her back for the second season. Unfortunately, the show was cancelled after the first season. Jordan McCoy explained to Popdirt.com, "Many people don't know this but the producers were actually saving Keke for the second season of [*American Juniors*]. So when they decided against another season, Keke started really focusing on acting." Keke was probably pretty disappointed that she didn't make it on the air with the show, but her time in L.A. really inspired her to keep trying. As the saying goes, when one door closes, another one opens.

Keke knew that if she wanted to be a successful actress, the best place for her to live would be Los Angeles. Since she was only ten years old, a move across the country would affect her entire family. The Palmers would need to relocate if she chose to pursue a career in Hollywood, and they would all have to give up their lives in Illinois. "I knew opportunities would pop up if I just kept on trying," Keke told Anthony Breznican at *USA Today*. "I talked it over with my sister, and I didn't have anything to bribe her. I asked her, 'Please?' I knew she was excited about going to high school and I didn't want to take that away from her — but I really wanted my dream to come true. She said, 'You're really talented, and I think this could be good for you.'" With L'Oreal's blessing, Keke convinced her parents to leave Harvey, Illinois, the bigger house they had just purchased, and their stable jobs, for Los Angeles. The Palmers moved to California in November 2003, just a few months into the new school year.

Once in California, Keke set up her schedule to meet the demands of auditions and work. Rather than enrolling in a new elementary school for one semester, Keke was homeschooled following Illinois education guidelines. Then her parents learned about California's Options For Youth program, and decided it was a better fit for Keke and her siblings. The program had enough flexibility for her to continue to work, yet was rigorous enough to ensure that she would not fall behind her peers. Education is very important to the Palmers, and Keke intends to go to college like former child actors Jodie Foster and Natalie Portman. In an interview with Scholastic News Online, Keke said, "Yeah, I definitely want to go to college. I'm thinking about going to Howard University and getting my Masters at Yale. If acting doesn't work out, maybe I'll be an anesthesiologist. They have a really good salary. All I have to do is get a little bit better in math and science." Homeschooling was the perfect fit for Keke. She was able to study hard, but she had lots of extra time to rehearse and work on her singing and acting skills.

It wasn't all work and no play though. The Palmers also wanted to make sure that Keke had time to have fun and hang out with friends. "Keke is a very social kid. Our main challenge with her is finding time where she can socialize with other children. We make sure she gets to some birthday parties, skating parties and movie outings with her friends," Keke's dad told Children in Film. Sharon and Lawrence are always quick to make Keke take a break if they think she's working too hard. They want to make sure she stays balanced, healthy, and happy. Her well-being will always be more important to them than her career.

The other major change Keke made when she moved to Los Angeles was to take on a professional name. She had been going on auditions as Lauren Palmer, but one day her manager overheard Sharon call her Keke. According to TeenVoices.com, Keke's manager said, ". . . you should change your stage name from Lauren Keyana Palmer to Keke Palmer." Keke's Hollywood transformation was complete, and she was well on her way to realizing her wildest dreams.

CHAPTER 2:
Breaking Into the Biz

Once Keke was in Los Angeles, her agent wasted no time sending her on auditions for commercials, television shows, and movies. Keke was enthusiastic and ready to take on Hollywood, and she couldn't wait to start working. Her very first audition was for a small part in *Barbershop 2: Back In Business*, the sequel to the successful film *Barbershop*. Keke blew the casting agents away and booked the role. *Barbershop 2*, directed by Kevin Rodney Sullivan, continued telling the story of a group of barbers who work in a family-owned barbershop called Calvin's on the South Side of Chicago. The film starred Ice Cube, Cedric the Entertainer, Sean Patrick Thomas, Eve, Troy

Garity, Michael Ealy, and Leonard Earl Howze, with a special appearance by Queen Latifah.

In the film, Calvin's Barbershop is a place for men from the community to drop by for a haircut, shave, and the latest gossip. One day, the barbers discover that a franchise barbershop is about to open up across the street from Calvin's Barbershop. The franchise shop is modern and fancy, and appears to be a competitive business threat. In fact, Calvin, played by Ice Cube, believes that he will be put out of business. So Calvin, his team of barbers, and members of the community band together to fight to save the barbershop, and to keep their neighborhood from being taken over by corporate chain stores.

Keke played the niece of Queen Latifah's character Gina and appeared in one scene. In the film, Calvin decides to throw a barbecue to show his customers how much he appreciates them. Eddie, played by Cedric the Entertainer, is in charge of grilling meat. Gina's niece shows up to the barbecue, and receives a burnt hamburger patty from

Eddie. She points out that the patty is burnt, but Eddie insists that it is just barbecued. When she asks why she can't have another patty, Eddie responds that it is free. Gina's niece refuses to eat the burger, and Eddie tosses it aside. This prompts her to inform him that she's going to tell her auntie. She returns with Gina, who engages Eddie in an entertaining battle of wits.

Throughout the scene with Cedric the Entertainer, Keke sparkled. She delivered each one of her lines with energy and conviction, and threw her entire body into the role. One moment she had her hand on her hip, delivering a sassy line, and the next she stuck her tongue out and rolled her eyes. It's quite clear that she was able to hold her own with Cedric the Entertainer, Queen Latifah, and Ice Cube, despite the fact that she was so young. Even though her scene was brief, Keke's appearance was important to the plot and character development in the film. She is memorable and charming, two characteristics that every star in the making needs in order to be a success. Keke's part may have been small, but it gave her a chance to work with some of the most respected African American actors in the entertainment industry. Keke must have been inspired getting to watch so many experienced and successful performers doing what they do best. Since Keke had grown up surrounded by strong African American role models, it was nice for her to develop some similar ties in Hollwood.

After landing that first role, Keke was red-hot. Word got around quickly about her talent and she soon landed a national KMart commercial and two television guest-star roles. The first guest appearance was on the police drama *Cold Case*, on an episode called "The Letter." Keke played a character named Arletta Marion, whose grandmother is murdered. The role was especially cool since Keke's scene was set in 1939! Playing her part with historical accuracy was a fun new challenge for Keke and she had a great time getting into character. The second role was on an episode of the medical drama *Strong*

Medicine called "Race for a Cure." Her character's name was Sarina. It was a small part, but the popular show gave Keke a lot of exposure.

After those small parts, Keke's agent felt she was ready to take on bigger projects, and sent her a script written by William H. Macy for a TV movie called *The Wool Cap*. The script was based on the 1962 film *Gigot*, written by and starring comic genius Jackie Gleason and directed by the legendary Gene Kelly. *The Wool Cap* told the story of a mute building superintendent, Gigot, whose past makes him unhappy — until he meets and befriends a young girl named Lou. Lou has her own share of problems since her mother has abandoned her, and the two lost souls instantly connect. With the help of an elderly tenant in the building, Ira, and a friend named Gloria, Gigot and Lou struggle together to overcome their problems.

As soon as she finished reading the script, Keke knew the role of Lou would be perfect for her. She told TNT.tv, "After I read it, I thought, 'I have to get this part. If I don't get this part, I'm gonna die.' . . . After my mom read it, she said, 'Keke, this is you. This is exactly you.' And my mother knows these things." Keke knew then that she had to convince the director, casting director, and producers that she was the right girl for the part. What she lacked in experience, she made up for in talent and hard work. Keke just needed a chance to prove that she was capable of handling a leading dramatic role.

Keke's agent sent an audition tape to the production company. Then it became a waiting game for the young actress. "We didn't hear anything for a while, so we thought we should just forget about it," Keke explained to TNT.tv. "Then my agent called and said I had an audition." Keke was psyched. It was a big step in the direction of landing the part she wanted so badly.

On the day of the audition, Keke realized that there were many girls vying for the role of Lou, and she recognized some of the other young actresses from other auditions in the waiting area. She knew it was going to be a tough battle to book the job. The thought of so many girls competing for the part didn't make Keke nervous, but the sight of William H. Macy in the audition room did, as Keke explained on TNT.tv, "I went in to audition and got so scared because William H. Macy was in the room." Luckily, Keke was a good enough actress to hide her nerves. There was no way she was going to let her nerves get the better of her. When she was done, she read lines with Macy.

Keke's audition was successful — she got a callback, which is acting lingo for a second or additional audition. In an interview for TNT.tv, William H. Macy said "We breathed a sigh of relief when [Keke] walked in the room during auditions." But Keke didn't know this — she had to wait to find out whether or not she had landed the role. "[I] didn't hear again from them for awhile, but I kept studying my lines in case they called me back," Keke recalled to TNT.tv. Her hard work and dedication paid off. One day, her agent called and told her, "They want you in Canada," which was where the movie was being shot. She responded with one word: "Hallelujah."

As soon as filming began, it was clear that Keke was the right choice to play Lou. The director/writer/producer of *The Wool Cap*, Steven Schachter, told TNT.tv, "What I love about Keke is she has this sort of urban, inner-city background. She's from Chicago. She's the real deal. She and her family just recently decided to move to Los Angeles and maybe take up acting. We did a nationwide search for this role. We knew she had to be good because she carries so much of the movie and we found the one girl, in this entire country, who could do it. It just has magically worked for her. We're very lucky to have her."

Keke enjoyed making *The Wool Cap*. "It's a very good movie," she said in an interview for TNT.tv. "You have to see it. If you don't, I'll be angry because it's really good." She especially loved working with William H. Macy. As she explained to TNT.tv, "It was really good because he's really humble. He's a very nice person and a funny guy."

After filming *The Wool Cap*, she said in an interview with Teen Voices Online that William H. Macy was one of her biggest acting influences: ". . . *The Wool Cap* was my first big role. During that whole film, [Macy] was just such a helpful actor and I really looked up to him after that. He was so nice to me and he gave me time. I really respect him for that and I could never thank him enough for giving me that role." Keke has a lot of respect for William as a person and as an actor, and she feels that she was very lucky to have gotten the chance to work with him so early in her career.

Keke had another exciting co-star in the film — a monkey named Crystal! Crystal played the part of Grace, Gigot's pet monkey in *The Wool Cap*. "Oh gosh, she's a kisser," Keke said on TNT.tv. "If you try to get her to come to you, she won't come. You just have to sit there quietly and wait for her. When she finally comes to you, she starts grooming you — picking things out of your hair and off your shirt. But she's really good."

The Wool Cap aired as a Johnson & Johnson Spotlight Presentation on TNT. Shortly after, Keke began earning critical acclaim for playing Lou. Her performance was so moving that she received a nomination for a Screen Actors Guild Award for Outstanding Performance by a Female Actor in a Television Movie or Miniseries. It was quite an honor. At ten, she was the youngest actress to ever be nominated for a leading role. Her fellow nominees included award-winning actresses Glenn Close, Patricia Heaton, Hilary Swank, and Charlize Theron. Glenn Close won the award, but Keke wasn't disappointed — she was simply happy to be nominated. "It was just amazing to be standing up there with them," Keke said in an interview for *The Making of Akeelah and the Bee.*

Keke's successes in 2004 led to more television work in 2005. She shot a pilot for a comedy called *Keke & Jamal* for the Disney Channel. The premise of the show was that siblings Keke and Jamal Stewart, played by Andre Kinney, who plays Cooper on *Hannah Montana,* move from Los Angeles to Ohio to live with their grouchy grandfather. The show didn't sell, but it established Keke's ability to take on a starring television role, and made executives at Disney aware of her star power.

In addition to the pilot, Keke shot another three television guest appearances. She appeared in an episode of *Second Time Around* called "Big Bank, Little Bank" as Sharlene, alongside Tasha Smith. *Second Time Around* was a hilarious show that ran from 2004–2005, about a couple that was married, divorced, and then married again. After that, Keke guest starred on an episode of *ER* called "The Show Must Go On," playing a girl named Janell Parkerson. The episode of *ER* followed Dr. Carter, played by Noah Wylie, on his last day at County General. Janell showed up in the emergency room with a wrist injury from a fall at school, and Carter attended to her. She was very inquisitive, asking Carter many questions about the hospital. Later in the episode, Janell's wrist was in traction. Her parents arrived as Carter was checking on her. Mrs. Parkerson asked Carter if he remembered meeting her before. He didn't, so Mrs. Parkerson filled him in: He treated her in 1994 when she went into premature labor. Carter delivered the baby, who was Janell! *ER* has been a popular show for years and is one of the longest running shows on television, so it was great to have a chance to guest star on such a well-known show.

The third television show Keke made an appearance on was *Law & Order: Special Victims Unit.* The episode was called "Storm," and Keke played a character named Tasha Wright. Tasha and her sisters were victims of Hurricane Katrina. They were kidnapped from New Orleans during the aftermath of the disaster. Throughout the episode, Detective Benson, played by Mariska Hargitay, is determined to get to the bottom of their case.

In addition to the television guest-starring roles, Keke landed a part in a television movie called *Knights of the South Bronx,* playing Kenya Russell. The film was directed by Allen Hughes, written by Jamal Joseph and Dianne Houston, and starred Ted Danson, Malcolm David Kelley, Yves Michel-Beneche and, of course, Keke.

Knights of the South Bronx tells the story of a man named Richard Mason who loses his job and becomes an elementary school teacher in the inner city. At first, he has trouble getting through to his students, whose lives at home are so tough that school is the least of their worries. Anita Gates at *The New York Times* wrote, "Mason finds a way to inject some hope and a sense of control into his students' lives. One day, Jimmy (Malcolm David Kelley) happens upon his new teacher in a park. He is starring in a chess demonstration, playing 14 games at once and winning. Jimmy is impressed. Mason explains that chess is like a war and that 'each piece has a certain way that it can fight.' He presents the idea to the entire class as empowerment: 'Suppose I told you kids you could rule the world, your own chunk of the world?'" Soon enough, all of Mason's students want to learn chess as well. Keke learned how to play chess for the role. She didn't really have to learn the game to give a good performance, but she wanted to really get into her character's head and be as believable as possible. All of her hard work really paid off. Her performance was very powerful, and just proved how far her acting skills had come since she moved to Los Angeles. All these commercial, movie, and television roles prepared Keke to take the next big step in her career — starring in a film.

CHAPTER 3:
S-T-A-R T-U-R-N

During her first year in Los Angeles, Keke auditioned for the role of eleven-year-old Akeelah Anderson for the Lionsgate Films production *Akeelah and the Bee*. The movie is about Akeelah's attempt to win the Scripps National Spelling Bee, a spelling contest for students in middle and elementary school. Every year, many students around the United States take part in this competition at their school. During a spelling bee, students stand on a stage in front of other students, teachers, and parents. They spell words like "pterodactyl," "eczema," and "narcolepsy." The winner of a school spelling bee gets to compete in a regional competition, which in turn determines which competitors get to go to the national competition. In addition to being featured in *Akeelah and the Bee*, the Scripps National Spelling Bee has also been the subject of an award-winning documentary called *Spellbound*, as well as a movie adaptation of the novel *Bee Season* by Myla Goldberg.

Most of the spelling bee competitors in the movie *Akeelah and the Bee* lived in wealthy neighborhoods. Akeelah, on the other hand, lived in South Los Angeles. Her school could not afford doors on the restroom stalls. She did not like going to class because the other students made fun of her for being smart. Director and screen-writer Doug Atchison had created a character that would require a young actress to be intelligent and vulnerable, yet tough.

The studio executives at Lionsgate told the producers of *Akeelah and the Bee* to, "Find Akeelah and we'll go forward," as the producers explained in an interview for *The Making of Akeelah and the Bee*. Without the right girl, there would be no movie. It was as simple as that. Everyone involved in making the movie knew that they had to find a very special actress to play Akeelah in order to get the green light — meaning permission to make the film — from the studio. Sometimes casting is one of the most difficult parts of making a movie, but the producers for the film were prepared for the challenge.

In order to find the perfect actress to play Akeelah, the production team auditioned hundreds of girls for the role. Keke stood out from the crowd because of her acting ability and her perceptive approach to interpreting a scene. During an interview for *The Making of Akeelah and the Bee*, Director Doug Atchison said, "Keke Palmer will tell you that I knew she was Akeelah from the moment she walked in the door — which maybe I did. I think we saw about three hundred girls and we had everyone do the speech that's in our movie. She was the only kid who moved her eyes back and forth as if she was actually reading something on the wall, because she was actually reading something on the wall. She was imagining reading something on the wall. And it was powerful the way she read it. So, I knew she was special, then." Keke's first audition led to a callback.

For Keke, the audition process was an emotional rollercoaster. "On the second to last audition, it was the producers and Doug in a room and the casting director," Keke told About.com. "We were all in there and there was a scene where I had to cry. I didn't plan on going in there crying, I just planned on doing the best that I could. When it got to the crying scene I was nervous so I just took that and changed it and made myself cry. I was like, 'Oh my god, what am I doing?' But I didn't let that mess me up. I just kept on doing it and crying doing the lines." Keke was right to trust her instincts. She completely nailed the audition and wowed everyone in the room. "When I shook hands with the producers, Doug stood up and hugged me and said, 'Thank you so much.' When I got out of the room I told my mom he said thank you so much and that meant, 'Thank you so much for making it easy to give you the part.' I believe that was what he was thinking. He says when I did that he had a huge weight lift off his back," Keke told About.com. When the executives at Lionsgate Films saw the footage of Keke's audition, they said, "She's it, we want to go ahead. Let's go ahead," as they explained during an interview for *The Making of Akeelah and the Bee.* Keke had beat out hundreds of girls to land her first starring role in a feature film. Keke was so excited. She found out right around her birthday, and it was, by far, one of the best birthday gifts she's ever received. "My birthday came right around when Doug told me I'd got the part," Keke told About.com. "He gave me a lot of spelling bee stuff. He gave me the *Spellbound* movie and the 2003 National Spelling Bee. A lot of spelling bee stuff came up around the time I got *Akeelah* so I did get a chance to see the 2004 National Spelling Bee." Like any good actress, Keke accepted the materials and studied hard to prepare for the part.

In addition to having to memorize hundreds of word spellings, Keke had to master spelling and jumping rope at the same time. In the film, Akeelah keeps time to help her spell words correctly. Her coach decides that she should jump rope while learning words as a surefire memory technique. "When [Doug] watched the National Spelling Bee, a lot of kids did some things," Keke told About.com. "Some wrote on the back of their number to see how the word was spelled or kicked their foot or did semi-circles. So Doug had to make something that was normal for the spelling bee but also subtle so people would know that it was something that nobody really does. I thought it was a smart thing to do and really worked for the movie." Lucky for Keke and the crew, she didn't have too much trouble mastering the skill of spelling and jumping rope at the same time. Otherwise, it could have meant endless takes to get difficult scenes right. "It was pretty easy for me," Keke confessed to About.com. "I'm tall and had to swing the rope over my head really hard [and] sometimes it would hit the bushes and stuff like that, but it was pretty easy to do it."

Keke's preparation, diligence, and attitude paid off. She impressed everyone on the set of *Akeelah and the Bee.* Actress Angela Bassett, who played her mother in the film, absolutely loved working with Keke. "She [Keke] is entertaining us on the microphone," Angela explained in an interview for *The Making of Akeelah and the Bee.* "She's singing a little bit, she's dancing, and Laurence looks at me and says, 'She's not just a ham, she's a honey-roasted ham.' I mean, she really loves it. She's not shy at all." Keke's love for entertaining really shone through. Every day that she was on set, she gave it one hundred percent — just like Akeelah gave one hundred percent to her spelling in the movie! "She is very much like Akeelah herself in a lot of ways. She's very very smart. Akeelah feels things deeply, as does Keke. I can't imagine making this movie without Keke," Doug Atchison explained in an interview for *The Making of Akeelah and the Bee.*

Everyone on set was impressed by the funny little girl with the big heart and the incredible talent. Despite being the youngest of the lead characters, Keke was undoubtedly the real star of the film. In an interview for *The Making of Akeelah and the Bee* Curtis Armstrong, the actor who played Principal Welch in *Akeelah and the Bee* said, "To watch her . . . sudden instant focus is something I haven't seen very often in child actors." Producer Nancy Hult Ganis explained what she loves about Keke in an interview for *The Making of Akeelah and the Bee*: "She has an amazing gift: an ability to sort of feel the characters." And director Doug Atchison confirmed in an interview for *The Making of Akeelah and the Bee* that, "We made the right choice. She is astonishing, what she can do at age eleven." Mike Paseornek, production chief for Lionsgate Films, liked Keke so much that he had her in mind for a starring comedy role, and was also in negotiations to get her a television show. At eleven, Keke was in demand as a serious actress, and respected by everyone she worked with. Angela Bassett believes that Keke has a long career ahead of her. "My hope for Keke is that she has room to grow as an artist," Angela explained in an interview for *The Making of Akeelah and the Bee*. "And that she's able to transition smoothly from being a young actress to an adult actress."

When *Akeelah and the Bee* began screening for audiences around the United States, Keke's performance received lots of praise and attention from critics. Major film critic Roger Ebert wrote on RogerEbert.com, "Keke Palmer, a young Chicago actress whose first role was as Queen Latifah's niece in *Barbershop 2*, becomes an important young star with this movie. It puts her in Dakota Fanning and Flora Cross territory, and there's something about her poise and self-possession that hints she will grow up to be a considerable actress. The movie depends on her, and she deserves its trust." Keke must have been pretty psyched when she read that review! Dakota Fanning and Flora Cross are both very well respected child actresses who have starred in a number of critically important films. Benjamin Strong at *The Village Voice* commended her performance, writing, "It helps that newcomer Keke Palmer nails it as the 11-year-old prodigy, avoiding cuteness and conveying more angst than all the pasty freaks in *Spellbound* combined. When she stands up to Fishburne — 'dictatorial, truculent, supercilious' — she's totally convincing as someone who relishes words, which is more than you can say for many of her Tinseltown peers." It was clear that critics loved Keke, and considered her to be among the best of the young actors working in Hollywood. And they weren't the only ones!

In addition to good reviews, Keke started receiving nominations and prizes for her performance as Akeelah. She was nominated for the 2006 Chicago Film Critics Association Award for "Most Promising Performer"; 2007 Broadcast Film Critics Association Award for "Best Young Actress"; and 2007 Black Reel Awards for "Best Breakthrough Performance." Later, she was nominated for, and won the 2006 Black Movie Award for "Outstanding Performance by an Actress in a Leading Role," the 2007 Young Artist Award for "Best Performance in a Feature Film — Leading Young Actress," the 2007 Image Awards for "Outstanding Actress in a Motion Picture," and the 2007 Black Reel Awards for "Best Actress." Keke was completely blown away by the swirl of awards shows. She had hoped that people would like *Akeelah* and appreciate her performance, but she hadn't been expecting awards! She accepted each graciously, knowing that she was taking some very big steps. She had been a working actress for a few years, but now Keke was officially a movie star.

List of Scripps National Spelling Bee Winning Words, 1925–2005

Are you thinking of entering a spelling bee? You might want to study the following 78 words. Each Scripps National Spelling Bee Champion spelled one of these words correctly to win the entire competition.

gladiolus

abrogate

luxuriance

albumen

asceticism

fracas

foulard

knack

torsion

deteriorating

intelligible

interning

promiscuous

sanitarium

canonical

therapy

initials

sacrilegious

semaphore

chlorophyll

psychiatry

dulcimer

meticulosity

insouciant

vignette

soubrette

transept

crustaceology

condominium

schappe

syllepsis

catamaran

eudaemonic

smaragdine

esquamulose

equipage

sycophant

eczema

ratoon

chihuahua

abalone

interlocutory

croissant

shalloon

macerate

vouchsafe

hydrophyte

incisor

narcolepsy

cambist

deification

maculature

elucubrate

sarcophagus

psoriasis

Purim

luge

milieu

odontalgia	vivisepulture
staphylococci	euonym
elegiacal	chiaroscurist
spoliator	logorrhea
fibranne	demarche
antipyretic	succedaneum
lyceum	prospicience
kamikaze	pococurante
antediluvian	autochthonous
xanthosis	appoggiatura

CHAPTER 4:
Jumping In!

In 2006, after wrapping *Akeelah and the Bee*, Keke landed a role in another film produced by funny man Tyler Perry called *Madea's Family Reunion*. She played a character named Nikki, a juvenile delinquent runaway, who has been in foster care most of her life. Madea takes Nikki in and helps her change her rebellious ways. The film was a good experience for Keke, allowing her to work with an all-star cast, and giving her the chance to work with Tyler Perry, who is one of the great African American figures in the entertainment industry. Tyler Perry has dressed as a woman to play Madea in a number of films. His films often tackle difficult social issues, but they do so with a healthy dose of comedy that fans absolutely love. Keke's role was pretty serious, much like her roles in *Akeelah and the Bee* and *The Wool Cap*. She was developing quite the reputation as a dramatic actress, which Keke thought was pretty funny. As she explained to Vibe.com, "I'm always a comedienne! Everybody thinks I'm so dramatic because of the roles that I play, but I'm really goofy."

After completing *Madea's Family Reunion*, Keke continued to nail audition after audition. In 2007, she was cast in *Jump In!*, a Disney Channel Original Movie, opposite *High School Musical* star Corbin Bleu. The film also starred David Reivers, Corbin's father in real life and in the movie, Shanica Knowles who stars as Amber Addison on *Hannah Montana*, and Laivan Greene. Keke had a blast working with cutie Corbin. As she told Blogcritics.org, "Oh, Corbin! I had a lot of fun with him. I hadn't known about him until they told me he was in *High School Musical* and I had to go watch it now to find out who he is. Working with him was awesome." Keke quickly became one of the biggest fans of *High School Musical* and Corbin Bleu. And Corbin became a pretty big fan of Keke's once he met her. The two had a lot in common. They both loved singing, music, and acting and they had a really good time working together on the film.

Jump In! is about boxing, double dutch, family, and friendship. Keke said in an interview for "Inside the Ropes: The Making of *Jump In!*" that the message of the film was, "Don't be afraid to be who you are. Don't be afraid to do what you want to do, no matter what people say." Basically, be yourself! The film follows Izzy Daniels, a young athelete played by Corbin, as he struggles to fig-ure out how to balance the need to please his father and his friends with his own desires. At the beginning of *Jump In!*, Izzy is training as a boxer at his father's gym. He is preparing for a huge championship, and will have to beat Rodney, a bully who attends his school, in order to qualify for the match. Along the way, he decides to help out his neighbor Mary, played by Keke, when she loses a member of her double dutch team by training with her and her friends. Though Izzy is genuinely interested in double dutch, he refuses to train out on the street for fear of being made fun of since many of the neighborhood kids think that double dutch is only for young girls, and Izzy won't commit to competing with the team. Izzy also doesn't want his father to know that he's doing a sport other than boxing, for fear of disappointing him.

Keke and Corbin began preparing for the double dutch scenes well before the film started shooting. She already had the basics down, as she explained in an interview for "Inside the Ropes: The Making of *Jump In!*" "When I was eight or nine, I learned how to double dutch with my neighborhood. When I heard I was getting the part of Mary, I started doing more and more with my friends. So when I got here, I could just go right into it and learn all the tricks and new things." Despite Keke's impressive double dutch skills, she wasn't aware that it was a competitive sport, as she said in an interview for "Inside the Ropes: The Making of *Jump In!*" "I didn't know like that it was so complex, and had actual rules and tournaments. It was a great thing to be a part of." Corbin had to do a little more work to prepare since he'd never done any double dutch before. "I started training back in LA. They taught us how to get in and out of the ropes, four corners, certain little tricks like that, and worked on them for about three weeks," Corbin explained in an interview for "Inside the Ropes: The Making of *Jump In!*"

One of the most important skills for the actors to master was the art of jumping in. If they couldn't jump in convincingly, no one would believe that they were capable of doing difficult tricks. Chris Emerson, a double dutch instructor who was a consultant for the film, explained how to jump in for "Inside the Ropes: The Making of *Jump In!*" one of the DVD extras of *Jump In!* "The person jumping in stands next to the turner. And they watch the ropes. They want to jump in when the rope in the turner's hand that is farthest away from them is up in the air. So when that back rope hits the ground and goes up in the air, the jumper follows it in. The turners count off for the jumper. They'll let the jumper know when to enter by saying, 'One, two, three, jump in!' You jump into the middle of the ropes and jump. The key to jumping is that you're keeping the same beat as the ropes. You can jump with two feet, or once you get the hang of it, jump with one foot at a time." To jump in correctly and accurately, Keke and Corbin needed to be observant. They had to really watch the rhythm of the ropes and pick the perfect time to make their moves. But they also had to really trust the people turning the ropes, because double dutch is really all about teamwork.

After the initial three weeks of training in Los Angeles, Keke said in an interview for "Inside the Ropes: The Making of *Jump In!*" that, "Then when we got to Canada, we started to really do tricks and really go into routines.

And we did that for about a month and a half. We were doing all these crazy things. But we also have doubles who help us." A very skilled stuntman named Marcus Taylor was Corbin Bleu's double, and he was responsible for a number of the dazzling stunts in the film. They left the really big, complicated tricks to the stunt doubles, but the actors did most of the double dutch work themselves. "I didn't just want to have them to do it," Keke said in an interview for "Inside the Ropes: The Making of *Jump In!*" "I wanted to do some of the stuff too." The actors worked on simpler skills like 180s, 360s, jumping in, and jumping out, before moving onto harder elements like the straddle entrance, which requires jumping over one of the turners to jump in. The training paid off; they were able to do a number of fairly difficult double dutch tricks, making their performances very genuine for the cameras. "We did push-ups. Donkey kicks — you jump forward on your hands and you jump back again on your feet. And then you jump back and forth in the ropes. Kips, you kind of lay on your back and you flip up on your feet," Corbin told an interviewer for "Inside the Ropes: The Making of *Jump In!*" Though it was difficult to master all the footwork and tricks at first, Corbin noted in the same interview that, "I think any new activity is challenging the first time you start. And dance really helped because double dutch is a lot of rhythm. It has to do with hearing the beat of the rope on the floor and timing your feet with it." For Keke, some of the tricks were harder than others — almost too difficult to conquer. "Only the push-ups!" Keke said in an interview for "Inside the Ropes: The Making of *Jump In!*" "The backflips too. Because those things you actually have to have muscle for to learn so quick! I mastered the push-ups, not so much the backflips." Even though she didn't really get the backflips down, it was still impressive just how many tricks Keke did learn in a very short amount of time! The choreographer for the film, Troy Liddell, said in an interview for "Inside the Ropes: The Making of *Jump In!*" that, "It worked out that the doubles were sitting down a lot longer than they anticipated." The routines Keke and Corbin did on film look dynamic and professional, giving a real sense of excitement to the movie. In addition to learning double dutch and acting for the film, Keke recorded a song for the soundtrack called "Jumpin'," and even shot a music video for the track.

One thing that Keke couldn't prepare for by training or studying hard was the kissing scene she had with Corbin in the movie. "I can admit I was nervous for the kiss in the movie — it was my actual first kiss," she confessed in an interview for "Inside the Ropes: The Making of *Jump In!*" "At the same time I was like well, it doesn't count! So it was all good." Keke hadn't had much experience with romance, but she put her acting skills to good use, and fans were really rooting for Mary and Izzy to get together by the end of the film. Keke probably didn't mind the romance too much since she did get to flirt with a total hottie like Corbin! After all, not many girls can say they got their first kiss from an adorable superstar.

The movie was a hit with fans and critics, which was great news for Keke. She had really loved making a movie for kids her own age, so she was glad that her peers enjoyed it. Keke had mostly worked in films and television aimed at adults up until *Jump In!* and she found that working on a teen movie was even more fun than she had expected. She had a blast hanging out with her co-stars in between takes and goofing off with them at the end of each day. But the best part, at least in Keke's eyes, was that *Jump In!* earned her a lot of fans her own age! She couldn't wait to do another show or movie that dealt with subject matter she could really relate to as a teen herself!

Tips From Double Dutch Instructor Chris Emerson on How to Start Training Double Dutch

- Find a teacher or instructor of double dutch who lives in the neighborhood

- Work at your own pace; don't rush yourself

- Work in a wide-open space where the ropes can't get caught on anything

- Wear comfortable clothes and sneakers

- Turning: Turning is equally as important as jumping. Chris says that, "If you don't have good turners, you can't do double dutch."

- Turning technique: Hands drawing large circular motions on the wall. Don't pull your hands away as you're making the large circular motions. As your hands go up, touch your thumb to your nose.

CHAPTER 5
Cleaning House

In 2007, after completing *Jump In!*, Keke continued working in television and film. She reprised her role as Nikki on the first episode of a new TV show from Tyler Perry. The show was called Tyler Perry's *House of Payne*, and the episode was titled "The Bully and the Beast." In the episode, Nikki is bullying Malik, one of the show's main characters. Malik's great-uncle, Curtis, has to meet with Madea, Nikki's foster mother, to work things out between the two. Curtis has been encouraging Malik to stand up for himself, but when Curtis meets Madea he's the one scared of her bullying personality. In the end, Nikki and Malik are paired up as study partners to help them learn to get along. Since Keke is so sweet in person, she had a lot of fun getting to play a bully. She would never bully anyone in real life, so it was probably pretty funny to watch her be tough and mean while the cameras were rolling.

Keke's next project was guest starring on an episode of the TEENick television show *Just Jordan*, starring Lil' JJ, Raven Goodwin, Eddy Martin, and Justin Chon. Her character was a teen pop star named CeCe Livingston. The guest stint was one of Keke's favorite jobs, since she already knew most of the cast. "I already knew Lil' JJ and I knew Raven Goodwin who plays his cousin Tangie on the show, so to finally be a part of that cast was a lot of fun," Keke told *VIBE*. She had a blast goofing off with her friends between takes and planning more time to hang out. Since she was already good friends with JJ and Raven, it was a very relaxed set! "I knew JJ, I went to his sweet sixteen, and then my mom is best friends with Raven's mom, so I know them pretty well," Keke explained

Keke makes her mark at Planet Hollywood in New York City.

Joe Corrigan/Getty Images

Keke hugging her **adorable** brother and sister.

Keke shares a hug with costars Ashley Argota and Matt Shively on the set of *True Jackson, VP*.

KEKE
belting out a
SOLO
for her fans!

KEKE at the 2008 Kids' Choice Awards.

Kevin Mazur/WireImage/Getty Images

Keke at the world premiere of *The Longshots.*

Jump In! costar Corbin Bleu
posing with Keke.

Dan Steinberg/AP Images

Keke shows off her style on the *Teen Vogue* red carpet.

to *VIBE.* Hopefully Keke will get another chance to work with her friends in the future.

Keke then turned her attention to film, accepting a role in *Cleaner,* a thriller starring Samuel L. Jackson, Eva Mendes, Ed Harris, and Luis Guzmán. Keke played Rose Carver, daughter of crime scene cleaner and former police officer Tom Carver, played by Samuel L. Jackson. One of the reasons that Keke was so excited about *Cleaner* was that she got to work with Samuel L. Jackson. He has had a very long, successful career full of exciting roles and Keke really looks up to him. They had most of their scenes together, and she definitely learned a lot from working with him. Another reason she was psyched for the film? Keke's character in *Cleaner* is very complex and challenging. She loves tackling tough characters and Rose was especially interesting for Keke. Director Renny Harlin told Creators.com, "Keke's character is hitting puberty and has a lot of issues. They have a strained relationship that's very much in the center of the whole movie. And, oh my God, she is so good." The film didn't do as well as Keke had hoped at the box office and didn't get that much attention from critics, but it was still a great addition to Keke's résumé. Her performance was fantastic and she made a lot of contacts working with so many big name stars!

In 2008, Keke had an opportunity to do voice work for an animated film titled *Unstable Fables: Tortoise vs. Hare.* The film was produced by The Jim Henson Company. They are the creators of the Muppets, *Fraggle Rock,* and lots of other beloved children's television shows and films over the years, so it was a real honor to work with them. Keke was the voice of Crystal Tortoise, and was part of a great cast that included Drake Bell, Chris Elwood, Vivica A. Fox, Adam Friedman, Danny Glover, and Jay Leno. It was Keke's first big voice-over role and she had a great time getting into the recording box and bringing her animated character to life. Doing voice-over is very different than live-action, especially since you don't really work with the other actors. Keke was alone in her booth recording her parts, so when she saw the finished product she was blown away! It was pretty cool to see all of the animation and finally hear what everyone else sounded like!

By the time she was fifteen years old, Keke had really done it all. She had been in plays, sung with her church choir, done commercials and voice-over work, guest starred on television shows, and was a bona fide movie star. So what was left for Keke to conquer? Plenty!

CHAPTER 6:
A Sure Shot

In 2003, while Keke was filming her first movie, *Barbershop 2*, a girl named Jasmine Plummer became the first female quarterback to play for a Pop Warner football team. Keke and Jasmine actually had a lot in common, although they didn't know it yet. Both girls were eleven years old at the time of their first great achievements. Jasmine grew up in Harvey, Illinois, which is the same town where Keke was born. And, of course, both girls are talented, driven, and unwilling to take no for an answer!

While Keke was singing in church, Jasmine was play-ing football on the street with her uncle Fred Johnson.

Uncle Fred was coaching the local Pop Warner team, the Harvey Colts, and encouraged Jasmine to play with the team even though most people consider football to be a boy's sport. But Uncle Fred didn't think football was just for boys. He knew that Jasmine could play and throw better than most boys her age. She had played linebacker and tackle for the junior peewee team and she could throw 65-yard passes on the football field! Practice after practice, game after game, Jasmine proved that she deserved to be on the team and playing quarterback, since she could out-throw every boy on the team. Her skills quickly silenced all the people who didn't believe that a girl could play football.

Before long, Jasmine led the Harvey Colts, which had a losing record until she joined, to the semifinals of the 56th Annual Pop Warner Super Bowl. Her performance on the field really impressed Shawn Moore, a former Denver Broncos quarterback and 1990 Heisman Trophy finalist. "I think Jasmine showed tremendous speed and agility," Shawn told EduPlace.com after the game. "As I stood next to three former NFL players, I saw her make several throws, and we all looked at each other in awe because the ball was so incredibly placed and well thrown." Impressing the pros isn't easy, which only goes to show just how great Jasmine is.

When the news about Jasmine's accomplishments hit the national media, film industry executives started calling Uncle Fred with offers to turn her story into a movie. Uncle Fred turned down every offer, until a project called *The Longshots* was brought to his attention. *The Longshots* was written by Los Angeles screenwriter Nick Santora, and portrayed Jasmine's story with sincerity and emotional depth. Though Hollywood was calling, Jasmine was surprised that anyone besides her family and friends would be interested in her story. She never imagined she would be the subject of a Hollywood film. "I love sports, and I just enjoy what I do. I was always taught to go after what I wanted and to be the best I could be," Jasmine told the *Chicago Defender*. "To me, it was just me doing what I loved and having fun with it."

With the right screenplay in place, all that was left was to find the right actress to play Jasmine. The actress would need to be spunky, talented, and have some serious athletic ability. After all, the audience would have to believe that the actress playing Jasmine was emotionally and physically capable of leading a football team to a national championship game. *The Longshots* director Fred Durst, of musical group Limp Bizkit fame, had one person in mind — Keke Palmer. In fact, Fred was so sure that Keke was the right person for the part that he took a meeting with her, rather than asking her to audition for the part. "Then I got signed on to the project," Keke told *Lee Bailey's EURweb*. "I just kind of had a meeting and talked about what I'd done and what attracted me to the movie. It wasn't like an audition-audition." Though Fred Durst was certain that Keke was the perfect casting decision, Jasmine wasn't completely sold on the idea at first.

"[Keke] looks too much like a girly girl," Jasmine told the *Chicago Defender.* "But when she pulled back her arm, I was convinced. She can throw a ball. I was very happy that she plays me. She did a great job. I can't see anyone else playing me like she did."

The admiration was mutual. Keke was very honored to play Jasmine. "It made me feel proud because [*The Longshots*] was based on a true story and football is considered a male sport," Keke explained in an interview for the Black Athlete Sports Network. Keke was very proud to be able to bring some girl power to the big screen, especially because she felt Jasmine's story would inspire other girls to go for their dreams, no matter how impossible they might seem. Keke told *ACED Magazine,* "This film is about a young girl who goes out and defies the ordinary by going on an all male football team and showing them that she can bring them to the top. That she has the guts and she has the power, even though she is a girl, to bring them to the top." And the role was even more special because it was the first role that she chose for herself without any influence from her parents or agent. "This is the first script that I have read on my own so I was really excited about learning it and getting into the role," Keke said to *ACED Magazine.* She went on to explain that she wanted to do the movie "Because it is a true story and how motivational it was to motivate young girls to go out for things even if they think they are not made for it just because they are girls. Also, because Ice Cube was going to be part of it." Ice Cube is an actor and performer that Keke really looks up to, so getting to work with him again was a dream come true for her!

After getting through the entire script and doing research for the role, Keke became a big fan of Jasmine's determination and never-give-up attitude. "The story is truly inspirational, and Jasmine did her thing," Keke said to the *Chicago Defender.* "While I like sports but really can't play football or basketball, I like that Jasmine didn't let anything or anyone stop her from doing it. Once you set your mind to doing something, you must keep going." Keke could really relate to Jasmine even though the two girls are different in a lot of ways since that's Keke's philosophy too! Keke has never let anything stop her from going after her dreams and she's been super successful because of it — just like Jasmine.

In order to be a believable football player onscreen, Keke had to train hard and learn the finer points of the game. This meant that she had to run drills exactly like the ones Jasmine would have done in practice. "I went through a month of football training, like one hundred balls a day," Keke told *Lee Bailey's EURWeb*. "I was throwing them, getting the mechanics and getting the footwork. I got a lot of muscles and now I'm even better with my athletic ability." Training was tough, but Keke actually found she enjoyed getting into top shape. "Working all day in the hot or the cold . . . it was just really hard for me," Keke told *ACED Magazine*. "I had never done anything that was hurtful to your body, but it was really stressing on your body." In the end Keke's legs were muscular enough to actually play football — and perfect for the stance needed for a quarterback. Keke told Kidzworld that, despite the pain of workouts, the football training "was a great experience, I had a great coach."

Keke's hard work and perseverance paid off. She can throw a football about forty yards, which is very impressive for someone who had never played football before the film. The final cut of the film uses many actual shots of her throws and plays, instead of relying solely on the work of a double. "I think that it was very rewarding that I got to play with the guys on the team," Keke explained on *Lee Bailey's EURWeb*. "They were so awesome and cool and fun." Not bad for a girl who claimed on *Lee Bailey's EURWeb* that she's "never been into sports that much."

Once filming began, Keke and Jasmine met for the first time. Despite their shared determination and drive to succeed, the two girls have very different personalities. Keke is outgoing and bubbly, and Jasmine is more quiet and reserved. "[Jasmine] was a very shy, quiet young girl," Keke told *OK! Magazine.* "It took me aback because when you think about a girl playing football, you think of somebody really strong, but she was just a regular girl, just like me. She was just playing a sport that she loved. She was a really nice, really sweet girl. She actually told me a story — when she first started playing football, the guys didn't believe that she would be really good. She just had to show them. The first game that she played, she tackled a guy and broke his leg. The guys were like 'we really get that you're amazing.' They realized she was there to play the game, not to play dress up. She really was there to play the game." Once Keke and Jasmine got a chance to talk and hang out they became fast friends, and talking with Jasmine really helped Keke get into character.

The Longshots is an adaptation, rather than a completely faithful telling of Jasmine's real-life story. The setting, characters, and certain plot details were altered for the movie. For instance, the town in the film is called Minden, rather than Harvey, and the football team is called the Minden Browns. Ice Cube plays a character named Curtis Plummer, who is Jasmine's uncle and coach in the film. Curtis, along with lots of other men in Minden, is out of work because the local plant was closed. Jasmine is a shy, reserved young girl who doesn't have a lot of friends. Her mom, Claire, played by Tasha Smith, needs to pick up night shifts to help make ends meet, but there is no one to watch Jasmine if she does. Claire urges Jasmine to join some after-school clubs, so Claire can work later, but Jasmine is bullied and teased at school and doesn't want to stay late. In the end, Curtis ends up babysitting Jasmine after school, and he helps her discover her love of football and her talent for the game.

The Longshots follows both Curtis and Jasmine's journeys. For Curtis, working with Jasmine allows him to reconnect with football, a sport he stopped playing when he suffered a career-ending injury. And for Jasmine, working with Curtis gives her confidence in her abilities as an athlete, and helps her get over her shyness. As Jasmine and her team win game after game, the town of Minden begins to get in on the excitement. Soon everyone in Minden has rallied behind Jasmine, and their encouragement and support help Jasmine go on to the championship game.

Keke enjoyed working with Ice Cube and Tasha Smith again, as she explained to the Black Athlete Sports Network that, "They are both great actors and I had a lot of fun working along with them." Keke also told Kidzworld that, "It was great to work closer with [Ice Cube] because in *Barbershop 2* we had like one scene together so it was definitely cool to get to know him better. He's so cool, laid back — definitely a family guy." And Keke loved working with director Fred Durst. "It was pretty cool [having Fred Durst as the director], he's definitely an artist," Keke said to Kidzworld. "It wasn't hard to see him as a director once I met him because he's such an artist no matter what field."

The real-life Jasmine stopped playing football when she reached high school. Her mother felt that it was no longer safe for her to be on the field with much bigger and stronger boys. Keke thought they made the right decision. As she explained to *ACED Magazine*, ". . . I think as my character Jasmine Plummer did when she stopped playing at thirteen, I think that is the right age. The guys get too rough and their bodies get bigger. And the girls, unless they work out, are pretty petite, and I don't think . . . the way that guys work and move in that type of sport . . . I don't think it is safe. I definitely think it would be cool if we had an all-girls team playing." Now attending Joliet West High School, Jasmine is a varsity player on the girls' basketball team and also participates in track and field. Her plans for the future are to play in the WNBA and become an athletic trainer. For all the girls who want to follow in her footsteps, Jasmine told the *Chicago Defender*, "My advice is to just do what you believe in and be the best. Be better than the boys. Just follow your heart."

CHAPTER 7:
So Cool

In a very short amount of time, Keke had really established herself as a superstar A-list actress. But, despite the fact that she was busy with television and film projects, Keke hadn't given up on her first love — she still wanted to pursue singing. "My mama sang, so I always thought when I grew up I'd be a singer, but acting kinda shot off for me first," Keke told *VIBE*. Keke was very vocal about her incredible voice and her love for music, and many people involved with her films took notice. "[S]inging came back up to me after I did *Akeelah and the Bee*, then Jimmy Jam and Terry Lewis, who did a song on the soundtrack of *Akeelah and the Bee*, told my mom that it would be good to try to get me out there and do an album and have movies come out," Keke told *VIBE*. Keke and her mom took that advice, and soon Keke had the opportunity to record songs for three movie soundtracks. She sang background vocals with Michelle Williams for Deborah Cox in "Definition of Love" for *Akeelah and the Bee.* That was especially cool for Keke since she had a song on the soundtrack for a movie she had starred in! Next she recorded "Tonight" with Cham for *Night at the Museum.* Then she got into the studio to record "It's My Turn Now" and "Jumpin'" for *Jump In!*

Executives in the music industry took notice. They knew that Keke could be an incredible pop star with her big voice and natural stage presence. And it didn't hurt that Keke had proven herself to be a successful actress that young girls really related to. As soon as Keke started shopping her music around, four major labels offered her recording contracts. It must have been pretty flattering for Keke to have four labels fighting over her. In the end, though, she chose to sign with Atlantic Records because she felt it was the right place for her to start her singing career. They offered her the opportunity to really be involved in the music-making process, from songwriting to singing. Plus Atlantic has a long history of producing legendary artists like Aretha Franklin and Ray Charles. So Keke knew she would be in good company.

Keke's debut album was special for so many reasons, but one of them was that it was the first professional project that Keke got to work on with her older sister, L'Oreal. Keke and L'Oreal teamed up with a songwriter named Toby Gad, who is best known for writing Fergie's song "Big Girls Don't Cry." Together, the trio wrote four songs for the album: "Bottoms Up," "Rainbow," "Skin Deep," and "Wake Up Call." The sisters had a blast writing songs and Toby did a great job of bringing their two voices together. "It was a lot of fun working with my sister," Keke told *VIBE*. ". . . she does good with melodies and lyrics and then I'm a good lyricist, I come up with good words. We're a lot alike in different ways. She actually likes a little bit more punk rock music than I do, but she does like hip hop as well, so it's a lot of fun to merge our genres together." The result was four totally fun songs that will get stuck in your head the first time you listen to them!

The album's subject matter pulled from a lot of Keke's experiences with fame, friendships, romance, and staying positive even in negative situations. She tried to stick to subjects that her fans could really relate to — crushes, school, and even frenemies! "I'd say one of my favorite songs to record was the song I did with Rodney Jerkins called 'Friend Me Up,'" Keke told *VIBE*. "I had just come from Shreveport [Louisiana] filming the movie [*Cleaner*] with Samuel L. Jackson, and we were just getting to the last couple of songs, trying to fit them all in, ready to close down the album, and we get this song from Rodney Jerkins influenced by my sister and me. We thought of this title, 'Friend Me Up,' because sometimes when you're an actor or a singer you meet people who try to friend you up and be your friend and, you know, be actors or make them movie stars too."

After all the recording was finished, Keke decided to name the record *So Uncool*. "I named my album *So Uncool* because it defies the ordinary, you're different from everyone else," Keke told PBSKids.org. "It's like, being uncool MAKES you cool, because you're different!" The album is filled with songs about being happy with your own particular quirks and funny traits. She told PBSKids.org that, "There's this one song called 'Skin Deep.' I just love that song so much because it basically means, love yourself. Don't try to fit in to what everyone wants you to be, just be yourself and be happy with it." Keke's music delivers important messages, in addition to being very catchy and memorable. Keke told PBSKids.org that the most important advice she has for girls is, "Just to love yourself."

So Uncool took Keke about a year to write and record. And at the end of that time, Keke was very proud of what she had accomplished. She hoped that people would listen to it and realize that she took singing as seriously as she took acting. "I think before people hear the album, they think, 'Oh, she's probably gonna be some teeny-bopper kid' and you know, 'I don't think she can sing' or 'I don't know if she can't sing' but I don't think they count on me being a true artist until they hear the album," Keke told *VIBE*. "A lot of people are surprised when they hear my CD, they're like 'Whoa man, you really can sing!' and 'This is some real R&B/hip hop music!' and so they're really surprised afterwards." Everyone at Atlantic had very high hopes for Keke's album. Unfortunately, Keke and the folks at Atlantic didn't always agree on everything about her album. They wanted to market Keke as sexy and urban, which is not at all what Keke wanted. She and her parents flat-out refused to record music that they thought was inappropriate for a young girl to be singing. Keke also refused to wear revealing outfits or be marketed in a sexy way, which caused a lot of arguments with Atlantic. In a letter posted on WhatAboutOurDaughters.com, Keke wrote, "From the very beginning Atlantic's A&R representative tried to get me to record inappropriate music, and my parents and I resisted." To help her work with her label, Keke and her parents hired DAS Entertainment to manage Keke's music career. But Atlantic wouldn't listen to DAS either. Atlantic wanted Keke to be "urban" with hip-hop songs with suggestive lyrics, and Keke was only interested in putting out positive music appropriate for a fourteen-year-old girl to listen to. Keke won the battle and her album was full of clean, upbeat music, but Atlantic won the war. They did almost nothing to promote Keke's album, and most customers didn't even know it had been released! Critics and fans who did get their hands on the album loved it, but Atlantic dropped Keke based on poor sales. Keke was very frustrated and hurt, but she had to keep reminding herself to stay positive. She knew that the right opportunity would come along eventually that would allow her to make the music she wanted to make.

A few good things did come out of *So Uncool*. Keke learned a lot about songwriting, recording, and the music industry as a whole. Plus, she got to do a few concert appearances that allowed her to really reach out to her fans. Keke performed at Arthur Ashe Kids' Day, an annual U.S. Open pre-tournament celebration. She also went on a thirteen-day tour with the Women's National Basketball Association (WNBA) to promote the album. During each game's halftime, she performed her songs. "Atlantic Records and I and [the] WNBA created a partnership with one another because I have a song called 'Footworkin'" that's going to be their theme song this year," Keke told PBSKids.org. "Basically, we talked to them about it and they let us promote 'Footworkin' and my record." After spending so much time in front of cameras, Keke enjoyed singing in front of live audiences. As she explained to

PBSKids.org, "It's good, because I like seeing people's expressions when they see me on stage. When I do my thing, I like to see how they feel about it. As a performer I like having an audience all the time!" While on tour with the WNBA, Keke got the opportunity to hang out with the players, which was incredibly cool since they are all such strong, independent, and accomplished women. "I played basketball before," Keke told PBSKids.org. "Not professionally, of course. But I'm playing on the tour! One of the players taught me how to do a right-hand layup. That was really exciting!"

One of the best things to come out of Keke's album was a partnership with Cherry Lane Music Publishing Co. Inc. They signed Keke to a long-term, worldwide publishing agreement. Cherry Lane is the publishing home to such artists as the Black Eyed Peas, John Legend, and Wolfmother. "I am so excited to be with a company that has so many amazing songwriters," Keke said on CherryLane.com. "I'm looking forward to working with the people at Cherry Lane for many years to come. Let's make hit music together!" The executives at Cherry Lane were psyched to have Keke join their roster. Richard Stumpf, Senior Vice President of Creative Services and Marketing at Cherry Lane, explained on CherryLane.com that, "Keke is an exceptionally talented artist with an impressive résumé; if she has accomplished so much at such a young age — we can't wait to see how far she will go in her music career." Keke's management team thought the move was excellent for her. David Sonenberg, President of DAS Communications told CherryLane.com, "Keke Palmer is a multi-talented sensation. She can act, dance, sing, and write. It's amazing how much she has to say at fourteen years of age. We are excited to be working again with the awesome team at Cherry Lane who can help us bring Keke's songs to the top of the charts."

The album came out on September 18, 2006, featuring the singles "Bottoms Up," "Wake Up Call," "Skin Deep," and "Keep It Movin'." Keke did get to shoot a video for the lead single "Keep It Movin'," which featured Big Meech. In the video, Keke is riding on a subway car. In some shots, there are two Kekes, each one wearing different style outfits. One outfit is shorts, knee socks, and a long-sleeved patterned shirt. Another outfit is a red striped shirt and a denim skirt. One of the Kekes is even wearing black and white checkered pants with a black and red checkered shirt! In another shot, she's wearing the cutest plastic, green star earrings. For Keke, each version of herself in that video represented a different side of her personality. "Yeah, that's all my different, you know, episodes of myself, you know? Sometimes I wanna be skater, sometimes I wanna be punk rock, sometimes I wanna be old-school hip hop . . . Sometimes I wanna be just regular old Keke . . ." Keke explained to *VIBE*. One thing is certain, every single Keke sings and dances and is every inch the star. Meanwhile, train cars and graffiti pass by in the background. The video is the perfect accompaniment to the song.

Keke believed that *So Uncool* would appeal to a wide range of people. "Young girls can listen to it," Keke told *Ebony*. "Adults can listen to it. I wrote four songs on it with my sister and a man named Toby Gad. Some of my earlier influences were Brandy, Aaliyah, Janet Jackson, Mariah, and TLC. So the CD has that kind of flavor to it as well." She also told PBSKids.org that *So Uncool* is ". . . just really fun songs for kids and adults. It doesn't have an age on it. It's really a good record." AOL Music agreed. They named Keke one of twenty-one musicians under the age of twenty-one, along with stars Rihanna, Taylor Swift, the Jonas Brothers, and Miley Cyrus. Keke's music debut may not have gone exactly as she planned, but Keke learned a lot and made a record that she was really proud of. She may not have topped the charts, but she stayed true to herself and her values. She also knows that next time she won't make the same mistakes. She's taking her time and choosing a music label that will really let her have full creative control of her music and her image and one that will promote her and back her up. Keke has never stopped believing in herself, and she's waiting for a label that believes in her the same way. One thing's for sure, her fans can't wait to hear more of her music, so hopefully Keke Palmer album number two will be on its way soon!

CHAPTER 8:
Keke Palmer, TV Star

Keke loves doing movies and guest starring, but she had always wanted to star in her own television show — preferably one that kids her own age would enjoy watching. After the Disney Channel pilot for *Keke and Jamal* failed to take off, Keke had put that dream on the backburner. But in 2008 Keke was given the opportunity to take another shot at television. While working on movies and recording her album, Keke heard that Nickelodeon was developing a new television show. The show was called *True Jackson, VP*, and was, in Keke's words to BlogCritic.org, "about a fifteen-year-old girl that gets a vice president job at a huge fashion company. And now she kind of realizes it's not that different from high school." Keke told *ACED Magazine* that True's workplace was pretty much like high school because "There are cliques, crushes, homework, bosses, and she realizes they are one and the same. It is about how she struggles and finds fun in both."

The show sounded incredibly cool, and was exactly what Keke had been looking for. "I heard about the role from a friend and thought it was a cool show and I would like to try out for it. So I had a meeting with the creator of the show," Keke told Kids.AOL.com. She could really relate to True; they were both teenagers with adult jobs. In order to secure the part, she even dressed the way she thought True would dress for the audition. "The audition process was really fun," Keke told *Blogcritics Magazine.* "I heard about the project and I wanted to read the script. I thought it was the most amazing thing I've ever read. It was smart and amazing. I wanted to be on it. So, I auditioned for the show. I put what I thought True's style would be all together. Luckily, they liked it and I got a call back and another call back and I got the part." Keke had landed the role of True Jackson, Vice President of Youth Apparel at Mad Style. She was the newly minted Nickelodeon star of a show that focused on fashion, friendship, and fun.

In the show, True is working a summer job selling sandwiches to different fashion companies when she is spotted by Max Madigan, the President of Mad Style. She loves how True had personalized some of his designs and hires her on the spot as his Vice President of Youth Apparel. It's a dream come true for True, who loves fashion and designs some incredible clothes. She and her friends take over the Mad Style offices, causing all sorts of problems, but also delivering seriously cool work. The rest of the cast included some very talented young actors including adorable actress Ashley Argota as Lulu, True's best friend and assistant; hilarious Matt Shively as Ryan, True's silly best guy friend; Canadian hottie Robbie

Ammell as True's crush, Jimmy Madigan, who just happens to be True's boss's nephew and the mailroom clerk at Mad Style. It also included a few very funny adults like Greg Proops as Max Madigan, True's zany boss; Danielle Bisutti as Amanda Cantwell, a snarky Vice President who dislikes having a teen around; and Ron Butler as Oscar, the receptionist and one of True's allies at Mad Style.

The New York Times wrote that True Jackson, VP is ". . . Ugly Betty for tweens — which means that the heroine is beautiful and cool but qualifies as an outsider because she's a fifteen-year-old suddenly thrust into a world of nasty, clueless adults." This description may be true of the pilot episode of the show, but as the first season of True Jackson, VP progresses, True begins to win over many of the adults in the Mad Style office, including an eccentric and difficult-to-please Icelandic designer. She is simply kind, polite, fun, sweet, inventive, and hardworking — the kind of person anyone would be honored to call a friend.

Fans of Keke's dramatic roles may be surprised at how funny she can be in a leading role on a sitcom. True is far more upbeat and confident than some of Keke's previous characters like Akeelah Anderson and Jasmine Plummer. But Keke has had a blast playing True because she relates more to True than any other character she has ever played. "I've always been really funny," Keke told *Blogcritics Magazine.* "I've always been a comedian in my family. I guess you can call me the ham. I've always been cracking jokes, doing that kind of stuff. Witty. It was kind of weird that I've always been the serious role. Playing comedy is a lot easier — not necessarily easier, but more natural — because it's always been what I have done." Working on *True Jackson, VP* has really allowed Keke to get down to her favorite parts of performing — entertaining her fans and making them laugh.

In addition to being the comic star of the show, Keke is also the writer, along with Toby Gad, and vocalist for the show's theme song, "True Jackson, VP." "I never was really confident in my writing at all," Keke confessed to Kids.AOL. com. "But it was just me there with producer Toby. I put my all into it and I worked really hard and finally got it to where I liked it. And I was really proud of myself because everyone really liked the song." Keke also told Kidzworld that, "It was pretty awesome to be able to co-write and sing the song for my own show." Fans love the song too, and Keke is hoping it will inspire them to download some of her other songs from iTunes.

One of the biggest challenges of taping a television show for Keke was filming in front of a live studio audience. Almost no one except the cast and crew are allowed on movie sets, so Keke wasn't used to having people just watching her perform take after take. But after a few episodes, Keke began to really love having the audience there. She told Kidzworld that having the live audience was "actually great because we get the energy pumping — when the crowd comes we hit it up an extra notch just because the energy in the room is so exciting and we want to give them a really great show." Fans who go to watch a taping of *True Jackson, VP* are never disappointed with Keke in the spotlight.

The cast of *True Jackson, VP*, has had a great time working with one another. "We always joke each other, but the chemistry's so great, so it's back and forth, back and forth, back and forth. I guess I couldn't ask for a better cast. We all get along. We're all like best friends actually," Keke explained to *Blogcritics Magazine*. Even with such a great dynamic, once in a while embarrassing moments still happen. One recurring element on the show is that True often bumps into other characters, sending colorful papers flying through the air and creating total mayhem in the office. But one time, Keke recalled to *Blogcritics Magazine*, "this one scene, this girl had dropped some water and I wasn't supposed to fall, but it accidentally happened and I fell on my face." Luckily the rest of the cast and crew didn't tease Keke *too* much about her fall!

Being a part of a Nickelodeon show has been a great experience for all of the young actors on *True Jackson, VP.* Ashley Argota, who plays True's best friend, Lulu, told *Blogcritics Magazine,* "Everyone is such a huge family here and I love it. We're all so goofy when we're recording. Keke and Matt like to play pranks. We have a great time. Keke and I are in school. Anytime we aren't working, we're always, always in school. And we go downstairs and rehearse and it's a lot of fun. It's magic. I love it here." Most of the classes are in the morning, and Keke told *Blogcritics Magazine* that, "Sometimes — Ashley will tell you — I'll be pretending I'm reading and I'll be asleep and my teacher won't notice." Life on set can be tiring, but taping a great show makes it all worth it. And Keke tries not to doze off in too many of her classes. Education is very important to her, so she studies hard to make up for the days she's too sleepy to pay attention!

True Jackson, VP debuted on Saturday, November 8, 2008, at 9:30 P.M. Eastern Standard Time to great success.

There have been some exciting guest appearances during the first season, including a cameo by skateboarding sensation Ryan Sheckler from MTV's *Life of Ryan* on the fourth episode. In that episode, True helps develop Ryan Sheckler's line of skater gear for Mad Style. Fans have loved the show from the very beginning. The premiere was the largest premiere for a live-action show in Nickelodeon's entire history and more fans tune in every single week. Nick knows they have a good thing and have signed up Keke and her friends for another season, so we can look forward to more fashions, feuds, and friendships to come on *True Jackson, VP.*

CHAPTER 9:
More Movies

Even with a hit TV show on Nickelodeon, Keke isn't about to slow her movie career down. She takes advantage of time off between filming episodes of *True Jackson, VP* to audition for movies and guest spots.

In late 2008, Keke starred as Jemma in an independent film called *Shrink* that premiered at the 2008 Sundance Film Festival and is slated to be released in 2009 across the country. "I have a movie coming out in 2009 called *Shrink* with Kevin Spacey and Robin Williams. And the movie is about Kevin Spacey's character. He's a therapist. My character just got over her mother passing. It's a dramatic role. So, we kind of talk and connect," Keke told

Blogcritics Magazine. *Shrink* was directed by Jonas Pate and written by Thomas Moffett.

Keke had a blast working with Kevin Spacey and Robin Williams on *Shrink,* as she explained to *Blogcritics Magazine,* "It was crazy [working with Robin Williams]. It was just crazy. Every time I think of Robin Williams, I don't think of him as serious. I always think about *Jumanji.* He can do something serious? It always throws me off in a way. Kevin Spacey's always a serious actor; knowing I was going to work with him was so exciting." Of course, Robin Williams and Kevin Spacey both delivered fantastic performances. And they were really blown away by Keke. They had seen some of her previous work, but they had no idea just how talented and professional she was and they were very impressed. *Shrink* was well-received at Sundance and it got a lot of folks in the film industry buzzing about Keke all over again.

Around the time that *Shrink* will premiere in theaters, Keke will be busy filming yet another movie. She has signed on to star as Roxanne Shanté in *Vapors*, a film about the legendary Queensbridge hip-hop collective Juice Crew. The Juice Crew were some of hip-hop's earliest pioneers and Keke is honored to be playing Roxanne. The rest of the cast is pretty stellar too. Evan Ross, son of Diana Ross, is set to play MC Shan, while Julito McCullum will play Tragedy Khadafi. There are rumors that Nas will play Kool G Rap, while David Banner will play Biz Markie.

Roxanne Shanté is rap royalty. She released a hit single called "Roxanne's Revenge" at the age of fourteen and helped bring hip-hop into mainstream culture. Keke was very excited to do the film. She told *Giant*, "[Roxanne Shanté] was fourteen when she recorded those songs. She had it in her contract that the label would pay for her to finish high school and college — that's inspiring." Roxanne Shanté grew up to be Dr. Roxanne Shanté, a mother of two who studied psychology and has numerous hip-hop and corporate clients. Dr. Shanté is currently very involved in working with urban communities, giving lectures on such topics as "Life After Hip-Hop," and acting as an ambassador to the United Nations. She's very much the sort of strong and powerful woman that Keke admires.

Of course, filming only one movie won't fill up all of Keke's time, so she's sure to be signing up more projects soon. And thanks to Keke's incredible reputation in the film industry, she really has first pick of most of the coolest projects coming out of Hollywood. Luckily, Keke has a strong sense of who she wants to become as an actress and, with her choice of projects, she can focus on movies that will really help develop her talents and push her into the next level of stardom!

CHAPTER 10:
Keke's Future

Considering how much Keke has accomplished in such a short time, you'd think she might be ready for a break. But not Keke — she's just getting warmed up! *True Jackson, VP* has been picked up for a second season, which is sure to be even wilder and funnier than the first. And Keke has her fingers crossed that there may be a *True Jackson, VP* made-for-television movie special in her future. Keke can't wait to see what the writers come up with for True to do next!

When Keke isn't busy filming *True Jackson, VP*, she plans to get to work on her next album. "Hopefully I can do another CD soon and things like that so I can get more of my singing out there," Keke told *Blogcritics Magazine.* Keke signed a new record deal with Sony Records and she's working to release her next album in summer 2009. Knowing Keke, the album is sure to be a blend of upbeat hip-hop and soulful R&B with positive lyrics. Her fans can't wait!

Of course, Keke won't be giving up her acting career for music anytime soon. She's going to be auditioning for new movies, and she's really hoping to take on projects that stretch her acting muscles and expose her to other incredible actors and directors. "I hope to start making my own films one day and have more lead roles," Keke told BlackAthlete.net. Keke would make an incredible director or producer, considering how much she has learned working on so many amazing films. But for now, she's focusing on acting. Keke has a lot to offer to any film, and directors know it! So you can bet they will all be fighting to get Keke signed on to their projects in the future.

Keke loves being an entertainer, but she hasn't forgotten about her education either. She's working towards her high school diploma and plans to attend college in the future. Keke is having a great time acting now, but she knows she may want to try something else in the future and having a college degree is the best way to ensure that she can chase any dreams that may come up.

One dream that Keke may want to chase soon is the possibility of designing her own clothing line. Keke plays a fashionista on TV, but she has some serious style in real life too. She's been featured in publications like *Teen Vogue* for her fantastic fashion choices, and she would love to bring her take on fashion to her fans. Keke is a little too busy right now to pursue this fashionable next step, but keep an eye out. You might find designs by Keke in a mall near you sooner than you think!

No matter what the future holds, Keke is going to be one busy girl in the years to come. She hasn't let anything slow her down yet, and that isn't likely to change anytime soon. With her passion, drive, determination, and talent, Keke is going to succeed at anything she puts her mind to. And with her big heart and imagination, there is no end in sight to what she will accomplish!

CHAPTER 11:
Behind the Scenes

Keke loves working. She's happiest when she's on set getting into character, working on her music, or learning new lines for a role. But even the busiest workers need time off sometimes. When Keke does take a few days off she tries to relax, but she usually has too much to catch up on!

Keke spends as much time as she can with her family, working or not. She and her sister L'Oreal are very close and the girls can spend hours talking about music, boys, and clothes. They write songs together and L'Oreal inspires Keke creatively every day. "I have an older sister who's eighteen and a younger brother and sister, they're twins. I get to see them often because they come on the shoots and we get along. My older sister and I used to get into fights and take stuff back from each other . . . It was usually my fault anyway, messing with her or being rude to her. Growing up solved that," Keke told PBSKids. org. Keke also makes sure she spends plenty of time with her younger brother and sister. Lawrence and Lawrencia are fraternal twins and they are two of Keke's biggest fans. And their big sis always makes time to play with them and encourage them to follow their dreams too.

Of course, Keke's parents love spending time with her too. They are her role models and she credits them with making her the smart, well-balanced young woman she is today. Sharon and Lawrence Palmer are always looking out for Keke's best interests and making sure that she stays true to herself and her morals. They go to church every Sunday, and even though Keke doesn't have time to sing in the choir anymore, she still loves singing hymns during services. And Dad always makes sure Keke gets nice home-cooked meals when she's not out on the road. "It's definitely hard on the road! You never get home-cooked meals because you're eating fast food. Whenever I'm home I try to slow it down and get a home-cooked meal. My dad's a cook, fortunately!" Keke told PBSKids. org. But even on the road, Keke does her best to stay healthy so she'll have plenty of energy for doing the things she loves. "It means a lot to me, because I'm always on the road doing a lot of things. So to be healthy is a major thing for me," Keke explained to PBSKids.org. "Like if I don't drink enough water, I will just pass out. Working all the time, if I don't eat healthy it can really do damage to my body." Keke wakes up at four o'clock in the morning most days for early call times or to prepare for meetings and auditions, so when she does have time off she tries to sleep in as much as she can!

Keke is lucky to have a few very close friends that understand her busy schedule and are always willing to see her whenever they get the chance. She's known Miley

Cyrus for a long time, although both girls are so busy that they rarely get to hang out anymore. ". . . She [Miley] used to live fifteen minutes away from me. We would just be hanging out, talking, singing on her little computer — you know, singing, playing around," Keke told *OK! Magazine.* One of Keke's closest friends is Tyler James Williams, who stars on the television show *Everybody Hates Chris,* and she explained to *VIBE,* "Okay, when I first met him we did not get along that good. But then the second day . . . He's like my best friend. We're, like, best friends. Like, the first day — we didn't hate each other — but like the first day when we met we were just like, 'Eh, whatever.' And then now we're like — I talk to him about everything! We're really tight."

Of course, Keke is closer with some of her friends than others. She wasn't allowed to date until she turned sixteen, but that didn't stop her from cozying up to one boy in particular! "I have somebody I like, but I can't have a boyfriend. My dad said I can't until I'm sixteen. My mom acts like he's my boyfriend. Like, if I'm down today she'd be like, 'Did your friend-boy say something to you wrong?' And I'm like, 'No, Mom! And sometimes if we're just hanging out and I'm in her room just watching some TV, she's like, 'Mmm, so what's up with you and your friend-boy? Are you gonna hang out with your friend-boy this weekend?' She knows that we like each other, she knows! My dad doesn't do that though. He's like, 'You've been hanging out with him too much,'" Keke dished to *VIBE.* Keke also told *VIBE* just how cute her friend-boy is! "He knows that he's really cute! He looks a little bit like Pharrell. He's not an actor. His dad is Creole and his mom is Indian, Italian, and black. And he has, like, really curly hair and I remember when my mom first met him, she was like, 'Whoa! You have good hair like that?' It was so funny! My mom really likes him and stuff." Sounds like Keke's friend-boy had the mom stamp of approval before she even officially turned 16. But her dad may have a little more trouble accepting that his baby girl is finally old enough to date! It's been very nice for Keke to have a close relationship with a guy who isn't in the entertainment business. She gets to take time off from being an actress when she's with him, and she knows that he likes her for her and isn't just trying to further his own career.

Who knows if Keke and her friend-boy will become an item soon, but Keke does know exactly what she wants in a boyfriend in the future. She wants a guy who is sweet, thoughtful, and who has his own dreams and ambitions. "I'd like him to be customized — to have his own style. Like Pharrell or Kanye West. They are their own person and have their own thing going on, and they are content with their own lives," Keke told *Ebony Magazine*. The boys better look out now that Keke is finally old enough to date!

Time off for Keke isn't all play and no work. She still has to keep up with her schoolwork to graduate by the time she turns 18. Keke studies every day on the set of *True Jackson, VP*, but she has to do homework and reading off-set. Of course, some subjects are more fun to study than others. ". . . My favorite subject is English. My worst is Math — and World History. I don't like them. In World History we learn about what's on the news and that's good, but to have to read those hundred pages, your eyes burn off. I'm tired," Keke explained to About. com. But Keke never gives up, even when she does get tired. Her education is very important to her so she tries her best at every subject, every day. She knows that the sooner she gets her work done, the sooner she can move on to fun things — like shopping!

Keke has a newly discovered appreciation for fashion. She's always liked clothes, but now that she regularly attends Hollywood events and walks the red carpet she has found her own style. She hits up vintage stores in Los Angeles to find unique accessories like cool jewelry and bags. It's a great way to spend an afternoon with her sister or friends, and she almost always finds something awesome!

In a lot of ways Keke is just like any other teenage girl. She studies, spends time with her family and friends, and loves to shop. She has to do chores around the house and follows her parents' rules (like no dating until 16!). But Keke isn't a regular teen. Her talent, determination, and work ethic have allowed her to get a head start on her career and to stand out from the pack. It's hard to imagine juggling a regular teenage life with a full-time career that just gets bigger and better everyday, but somehow Keke manages it all. She works hard everyday to achieve her dreams, and, at only sixteen, she has already managed to build the life of her dreams for herself. What could be cooler than that?

CHAPTER 12:
Becoming Keke

Being an actress can be hard work. Playing someone else believably takes a lot of talent. Keke has the ability to put herself into someone else's shoes and deliver a performance that feels genuine and real. She is able to bring an emotional depth to every girl she plays, and give even the quietest character strength and the spark of genius.

Do you want to know which one of Keke's characters you are most similar to? Take this "Becoming Keke" quiz to find out!

1. **You and your best friend have a huge fight on IM. How do you handle it?**

   a. You call her back immediately—after all, friends need to communicate in order to keep a friendship going strong.

   b. You spend some time alone to cool off, then find your friend and apologize for the fight.

   c. You automatically assume the fight was your fault, until someone else tells you that you were actually right.

   d. You stubbornly remain angry, until another friend helps you see your BFF's point of view. Then you apologize.

   e. A huge fight with your best friend? Not likely!

2. **After high school, what do you plan to do?**

   a. Continue working at your fabulous job

   b. You haven't considered going to college, but your recent academic successes have you looking at schools

   c. Attend college on a sports scholarship

   d. Find a university that will encourage your leadership qualities

   e. Study at Howard University

3. Your extracurricular activities include:

   a. Baking, spending time with friends and family

   b. Playing word games

   c. Track and field

   d. Double dutch

   e. Hanging out with friends, reading, and playing computer games

4. When you grow up, you would like to be a(n):

   a. Executive in the fashion industry

   b. Professor of literature

   c. Basketball star in the WNBA

   d. Manager. You are great at encouraging people to reach a tough goal.

   e. Oscar-winning actress and Grammy-winning singer

5. How would you most like to spend your summer vacation?

   a. Working at the job of your dreams

   b. Reading the dictionary and playing Scrabble

c. Trying a new sport

d. Eating ice cream and practicing new double dutch tricks

e. Recording an album

6. How would your friends describe you?

a. Kind, generous, and artistic

b. Smart, brave, and slightly insecure

c. Shy and strong

d. Upbeat, focused, and a total dreamer

e. Intelligent, amazing, talented, and cool

If you selected "A" for the majority of your answers, you are most like True Jackson.

Keke's character True Jackson is a teenage vice president of a major fashion company. True is warm, kind, inventive, and imaginative. It's her talent for fashion, as well as her willingness to work hard, that lands her a fantastic job doing what she loves. True is an excellent friend. Her best friend, Lulu, becomes her assistant after she lands the vice president position, and her friend Ryan is constantly in her office because he wants to spend his summer hanging out with her. She's just that cool!

If you answered mostly A's then chances are you like to do a good job on any project you begin. And even when you are competing for something you want really badly, you are highly considerate of other people's feelings. You would never cross a friend or even a frenemy to get what you want, no matter how much you wanted it. For True, friendship and doing the right thing is far more important than hogging the spotlight.

True is constantly facing deadlines, difficult personalities, and tough decisions at her job. No matter how stressful a deadline may be or how mean her coworkers may get, she never loses her cool. And she is always kind, even when someone is being unreasonable with her.

Keke had a lot to say about True, whom she described as "very optimistic and nice and kind of outgoing and kind of really funny." She told the *NY Daily News* that,

"True is a lovely person and very fashionable. True loves fashion, I absolutely love fashion. I love clothes and shoes and shopping, I absolutely love it. She's very productive. She's a perfectionist. Those are all my qualities. I saw myself in that character."

If you selected "B" for the majority of your answers, you are most like Akeelah Anderson.

Keke's character Akeelah Anderson from the film *Akeelah and the Bee* is a brilliant kid who succeeds despite all the problems in her life. Akeelah's home life may not be the best, but she deals with it by playing word games and spending time with her best friend. If you answered mostly B's, then you have probably risen above adversity too. You are willing to jump into unfamiliar situations in order to do something you love a lot.

As she studies for the spelling bee, Akeelah begins to believe in her abilities. She starts to follow her dream, even though it seems unreachable. She travels to another city on a public bus just to practice spelling with friends and to learn more about the spelling bee world. She asks a scary professor who lives in the neighborhood to coach her, even though she doesn't get along with him at first. Akeelah takes risks, even though they may make her feel uncomfortable at first. Her willingness to push herself out of her comfort zone pays off in a big way. You are probably a risk taker too.

If you selected "C" for the majority of your answers, you are most like Jasmine Plummer.

Jasmine Plummer from *The Longshots* exemplifies the characteristics of strength, tenacity, bravery, and loyalty. Though she is shy, she is able to put her shyness aside to excel at football and help her team win. She is also willing to put up with teasing in order to do something she is very passionate about. Even though no one believes that a girl can play football, she leads her team to a major championship game. She combines athletic prowess with scholastic success. If you chose "C" for the majority of your answers, you are probably a smart, tough leader.

Keke really enjoyed playing Jasmine, even though their personalities are quite different. "I am not as shy as her. My parents always made sure I believed in myself and I have never been afraid to go out for things. I have always been out to redefine ordinary and showing people that I can do anything," Keke told *ACED Magazine*. You are probably a quiet, but steadfast leader whose strength inspires others everyday — just like Jasmine.

If you selected "D" for the majority of your answers, you are most like Mary Thomas.

Keke's character Mary Thomas from *Jump In!* is a leader. Mary is the kind of person who sets a goal, and works her way toward it with incredible drive and determination. In *Jump In!*, she wants to win a major double dutch competition, and she believes that she and her friends are capable of doing just that. Sometimes she can be a little stubborn, but in the end she will stop and listen to a friend who is giving good advice. If you chose "D" for the majority of your answers, you are a natural leader who is able to put aside personal problems in order to achieve an important goal.

Mary is fun to hang out with, and a really good listener. She's the kind of friend whom you can tell all your problems and secrets, and you know that she'll never breathe a word of it to another person. Even when she's a little down, she radiates optimism. She's the kind of girl you want on your team to motivate you, and to tell you if you're acting inappropriately — she's a friend to the end.

If you selected "E" for the majority of your answers, you are most like Keke Palmer.

Keke is a gifted actress and singer. Despite her numerous awards and the critical attention she receives, she's still a humble girl who's not afraid to work hard. Keke will never slack off on anything! Whenever she meets a challenge, whether it's a difficult script or a complicated song, she faces it head on and never, ever backs down. In fact, Keke has probably never uttered the phrase "I can't do it." She has a total can-do attitude. If you chose "E" for the majority of your answers, you are probably a hard worker, an unstoppable force, and an immensely talented performer!

In a very short period of time, Keke has worked her way from reality television and commercials to starring in films and recording albums. She's not afraid to tackle tough projects, or try new things. She moved all the way to Los Angeles in order to pursue her dreams of performing. That was a very big sacrifice to make for someone so young. When asked "If you could clone yourself twice, what would the two clones be doing?" Keke responded to *VIBE*, "Okay, one is going to be eighteen, and one is going to be sixteen. The fourteen-year-old would be doing what I'm doing, of course, but the 16-year-old would probably still be living in Chicago, living out my life there, and if I was eighteen I'd be in California and I'd have a boyfriend." Keke knows that she doesn't have a normal life, but she's very grateful for all that she has been blessed with. And she wouldn't trade what she's accomplished for anything, even if she does miss being normal every once in a while!

CHAPTER 13:
Just the Facts

So, think you're one of Keke's biggest fans? You've listened to *So Uncool* hundreds of times on your iPod, watched all Keke's music videos on YouTube, you can spell every word Keke learned to spell for *Akeelah and the Bee*, and you never miss an episode of *True Jackson, VP*, right? Well here are all the facts that every Keke fan should know by heart!

Name: Lauren Keyana Palmer

Birthday: August 26, 1993

Star Sign: Virgo

Birthplace: Harvey, Illinois

Hometown: Robbins, Illinois

Mom: Sharon Palmer

Dad: Lawrence Palmer

Siblings: older sister, L'Oreal, and twin younger sister and brother, Lawrencia and Lawrence

Pets: an adorable dog named Rusty

Hair Color: Black

Eye Color: Dark Brown

Home: Los Angeles, California

Management: DAS Communications

Company that Keke wishes she could run: Juicy Couture

Favorite School Subject: English

Favorite Sport: Football

Favorite Colors: Pink, purple, orange, red, black, and white

Favorite Foods: Pizza, Bacon Cheeseburger and Fries

Favorite Restaurant: Denny's

Favorite Actress: Angela Bassett

Favorite Actor: Will Smith

Favorite Musicians: Beyoncé, Aaliyah, TLC, Brandy

Favorite Book: *Everlost* by Neal Shusterman

Favorite Gadget: Cell phone

Favorite Computer Games: Diner Dash, Burger Island, Cooking Time

Favorite Video Games: Mario Bros., Pac-Man, Tekken, Mortal Combat, and Wii Sports

Favorite Movie: *The Notebook*

Favorite Holiday: Valentine's Day

Favorite Song from Her Debut Album, *So Uncool*: "Bottoms Up"

Personal Style: Hip-hop meets vintage

Hobbies: Talking on the phone, talking to friends on the computer, going to the movies, playing food-oriented computer games

College Plans: Wants to attend Howard University for her bachelor's degree and Yale University for her master's degree

Literary Characters She'd Like to Play in the Film Adaptations: Meg from *A Wrinkle in Time* by Madeleine L'Engle, Jo from *Little Women* by Louisa May Alcott, Stargirl from *Stargirl* by Jerry Spinelli

CHAPTER 14:
Dress for Success

Keke has described her personal style as "hip-hop meets vintage" during interviews, and she definitely knows herself — her style is edgy and girlie at the same time. She wears a mix of graphic tees, stilettos, denim, sneakers, and silk dresses, effortlessly pulling off lots of different looks for different events. She's attended movie premieres in a variety of outfits. For example, she's been spotted in a delicate pink skirt, layered tank tops, and flip-flops; a silk blouse, skinny jeans, and knee-high boots; and a teal satin strapless dress with a bold black sash and heels. In fact, Keke is so cool that she can even rock looks that no one would ever expect — like a delicate cream evening gown and glasses with thick black frames for the red carpet. Fearless Keke totally pulled it off, looking sophisticated and beautiful! Have you ever wondered just what the secret to Keke's fashionable style is? It's simple. Keke knows that fashion is about taking risks and trying new looks. She knows what works for her, so you won't catch her wearing something that doesn't fit her well. But Keke isn't afraid to try a bold pattern or a statement accessory (like glasses!) if she thinks it looks good, even if no one else is wearing anything like it.

Of course, a fashionista like Keke does have a few signature looks that are classic and timeless. So if you want to score style like Keke's, there are a few wardrobe basics that are must-haves! Remember — "hip-hop meets vintage" isn't exactly mainstream. You may already have some of the following pieces in your closet, or you can find that elusive item at your favorite thrift store. The most important thing to remember is that being stylish doesn't mean you have to spend a lot of money or buy expensive designer brands.

Black open-toe heels

Whether you're going casual or dressing up, you can't go wrong with a pair of black peep-toe pumps. You can dress up a T-shirt and jeans with black open-toe heels, or pair them with a knee-length cotton or silk dress for a more polished look. Keke wore slim-fitting black pants, a turquoise blouse, and black open-toe heels to the 40th NAACP Image Awards Press Conference.

Jewel-tone shirts and dresses

Bright colors will definitely help you stand out in a crowd. But choosing the right color can be tricky. Jewel tones like deep turquoise, royal purple, and dark, rich green look great with every skin color! So forget dreary grays and gloomy blacks: add ruby, emerald, and sapphire hues to your wardrobe to really brighten up your look! Keke wore an amethyst-colored tank dress to the Kids' Inauguration and shone on television and in photographs from the event.

Earth-tone flip-flops.

A pair of brown or beige flip-flops made of leather or faux-leather can make any summer outfit look polished and help you keep your cool. These casual chic shoes are a must-have for laid-back looks and they are perfect for showing off a cute pedicure! Plus, the flat soles are comfortable if you are going to be doing lots of walking — like strolling the stretch of red carpet from a limo to the entrance of a movie theater! Keke wore a pink skirt, white tank, vest, and leather flip-flops to promote her film *The Longshots* in New York City.

Tank tops

Keke loves tank tops! She has tanks with V-necks, scoop necks, boat necks, and halters in a whole rainbow of colors. She pairs hers with shorts, jeans, and skirts and sometimes layers several tanks together for a casual look. She wore a white tank top with several white bead necklaces and had her hair up in a chignon for some promotional photographs.

Skinny jeans

Skinny jeans are one trend that is here to stay. They are very versatile and a staple in Keke's wardrobe. She wears hers hanging out with friends, going out to dinner, and even studying at the library. Paired with heels or boots, these jeans make legs look longer and leaner — and who doesn't want that? Keke rocks skinny jeans, a yellow shirt, and black-and-white, peep toe platform heels on the cover of her album *So Uncool*.

High-top sneakers

The high-top sneaker is the foundation of hip-hop meets vintage sportswear style. The shoe, which was popular in the 1980s and early 90s, has made a comeback in certain fashionable circles. Tons of stars can't live without their high-tops or Converse sneakers, and Keke is one of them. She wears her white high-tops with skinny jeans and a simple knit top for a funky, old school look.

Black knee-high boots

Black knee-high, heeled boots are a winter-must for Keke. They are perfect worn over skinny jeans or leggings, but also look great with dresses and skirts. They make Keke's legs look super long, and they're warm! Keke often wears her knee-high boots with skinny jeans and colorful silk blouses.

Striped shirts

Don't listen to the people who say that horizontal stripes are a no-no! Keke looks adorable in stripes and loves this fun pattern. She likes to mix it up and has blouses with thin stripes and T-shirts and polos with thicker stripes. Keke wore a red and white striped shirt with a flared denim skirt and white and peach heels to the Los Angeles premiere of *Hairspray*.

Graphic T-shirts

A graphic tee with a cool pattern or a funny saying is the perfect way to add some fun funk into an outfit. Whether you are wearing jeans, shorts, or a skirt, a graphic T-shirt can add a little edge to your look. Keke wore a yellow graphic tee and skinny jeans to a Screen Gems premiere.

Strapless dresses

One of Keke's signature red carpet looks is the strapless dress. A tasteful strapless dress looks polished and sophisticated for formal events. It's a very feminine look, and sometimes it's fun to be extra-girly! Keke wore a strapless beige dress with a black lace overlay and a black ribbon belt to the *Akeelah and the Bee* Los Angeles premiere.

CHAPTER 15:
Keke Online

Keke Palmer is one busy girl! She's constantly on the go, filming, recording, giving interviews, hanging out with friends, reading scripts, and catching up on homework. One day she's in Los Angeles, rushing from audition to audition, and the next she's off in Canada shooting a movie. The only way to really keep up with Keke is to follow her comings and goings on the Internet. You'll find up-to-the-minute information and news about all things Keke on the following Web sites.

www.kekepalmer.com

The Official Site of Keke Palmer

Like the name says, this is Keke's official Web site. Her latest news, links, and videos are all in one place. Get clicking!

www.nick.com/shows/truejacksonvp

True Jackson, VP, Nickelodeon Web site

Here's a site with everything you want to know about Keke's television show, *True Jackson, VP.* Find out more about the story, characters, and actors. As well, you can watch videos, play games, and download icons, wallpapers, and screensavers.

www.imdb.com/name/nm1551130

Keke Palmer, Internet Movie Database Page

Find out about Keke's latest film and television projects here. You can read about movies that are in production or soon to be released, and look at her complete list of acting credits.

http://www.akeelahandthebee.com/

Akeelah and the Bee Web site

On this Web site, you can download *Akeelah and the Bee* AIM icons and wallpaper, send e-cards to friends, and play word games inspired by the film. I-T I-S F-U-N!

http://true-jackson.org/

Keke Source Online

This site is a great resource for all things Keke Palmer. There is a forum where you can chat about your favorite Keke movie or song. As well, there are links to the latest Keke articles and videos.

Always check with your mom or dad before signing online. Keke would want you to be safe while surfing the Internet. Never give out personal information like your name, address, school, or neighborhood. And never, ever agree to meet anyone from the Internet in person. Keep in mind that not everything posted online is true. Some people with blogs and Web sites make up information to get attention. So unless your news comes from an official site, take it with a grain of salt!

Finally, if you can't find your favorite Keke site, don't worry. Web sites come and go all the time. So keep an eye out — a new Keke site may appear at any moment, with fresh facts and the latest gossip!